WITH ANY WALK IN NATURE,
ONE RECEIVES FAR
MORE THAN HE SEEKS.

—JOHN MUIR, NATURALIST

. . . DID SOMEONE SAY
WALK!?

—SYDNEY, DOG

T H E
TRAIL HOUND'S
H A N D B O O K

Your Family Guide To Hiking With Dogs

Ellen Eastwood

 WILDERNESS PRESS ... *on the trail since 1967*

The Trail Hound's Handbook

1st EDITION 2012
Copyright © 2012 by Ellen Eastwood

All interior and back cover photos, except as noted on page 71, by Ellen Eastwood, family, and friends
Front cover photo © Alaska Stock/Alamy
Cover design: Scott McGrew
Interior design: Ellen Eastwood
Editor: Amber Kaye Henderson
Veterinary Consultant: Emily Boothroyd, DVM

Library of Congress Cataloging-in-Publication Data

    Eastwood, Ellen.
      The trail hound's handbook : your family guide to hiking with dogs /
    Ellen Eastwood. -- 1st ed.
       p. cm.
    Includes index.
    ISBN-13: 978-0-89997-703-4
    ISBN-10: 0-89997-703-0
    1. Hiking with dogs. 2. Family recreation. I. Title.
    SF427.455.E37 2012
    796.51--dc23
                     2011047236

Manufactured in the United States of America

Published by: **Wilderness Press**
             c/o Keen Communications
             PO Box 43673
             Birmingham, AL 35243
             (800) 443-7227
             info@wildernesspress.com
             www.wildernesspress.com

Visit our website for a complete listing of our books and for ordering information.

Distributed by Publishers Group West

Disclaimer
The Trail Hound's Handbook is designed to engage and encourage the young dog owner to hike and explore nature with his or her pet at his or her side. It is not intended to be a comprehensive hiking and/or pet care guide. As with all outdoor activities, and especially those involving dogs, the full responsibility for safe practices and supervision belongs to the adult dog owner/parent. Wilderness Press/Keen Communications and the author in no way accept liability for any direct or indirect consequences that arise from following suggestions made in this book; readers are advised to use their own personal judgment.

HikingWithDogs.net

To my faithful pack,
who has remained at my side
for the length of this expedition,
without a whimper.

CONTENTS

CHAPTER 1

Unleash the Inner Trail Hound

The Call of the Wild

A lot has changed in the 15,000-plus years since that first "domestic" canine sidled up to his human and with patient, soulful eyes begged for a treat.

Or has it?

Today, more than 400 different dog breeds exist worldwide (not all breeds are officially recognized). Yet down to the last Peekapoo and Chihuahua, pureblood and mixed breed alike, every dog can trace its lineage back to the earliest wolves. It's no mystery, then, why every breed, every size, everywhere,

Every Dog Begs to Go Outside!

SCIENTISTS NOW BELIEVE THAT APPROXIMATELY 95% OF ALL DOGS DESCENDED FROM JUST THREE ORIGINAL FEMALES. *

Acting on Instinct

No amount of breeding or training can completely erase the numerous instinctive behaviors and characteristics written into your dog's DNA. In one way or another, these actions contributed to the survival of your dog's ancestors in the wild.

How many of these habits do you see your best friend repeating every day? What purpose do you think they serve wild mammals?

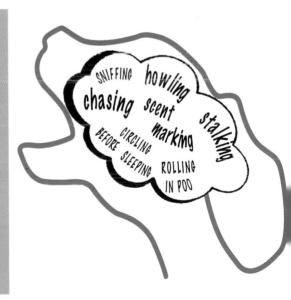

sniffing howling
chasing scent
circling marking stalking
before sleeping rolling
in poo

*Christine McGourty, "Origin of Dogs Traced," BBC News (2002).

Your dog responds to nature's call, and then stands to his full height and paws the ground furiously, grass flying, as he wipes his feet. Compulsive hygiene?

Actually, it's instinct. For his wilder ancestors, this routine was another way to mark territory, using the scent/sweat glands in the pads of their feet. This primal instinct establishes your dog's turf.

Plus, it makes even the smallest Chihuahua look large and in charge.

Prepare to Walk on the Wild Side

Social, territorial, predatory—any of your dog's naturally inherited Canidae family traits can be intensified by the stimulation of an outdoor environment. That's why, in your early wilderness adventures together, you should never assume that you know exactly how your dog will behave. Prepare yourself by mastering basic dog obedience skills. Practice, praise, and repeat.

Fido, an enduring favorite among dog names, comes from the Latin word for "faithful" or "fidelity."

With preparation, consideration, and a few choice tricks, this guidebook can give your pack the confidence to set out on new adventures and enjoy countless hours of discovery on the trail.

CHAPTER 2

YOU SCRATCH HIS BACK . . .

Does your dog get enough exercise? Has it been weeks since he's chewed on a good problem? Is he begging for more time at your side? Take your dog hiking! Every shared adventure promises more than just an afternoon of fun.

Chewing, Barking, Marking, Grazing, and General Mayhem

Misbehavior from good dogs (and they're all good dogs) is most often a sign of loneliness, boredom, frustration, or feelings of neglect.

Ironically, daily exercise and togetherness may be all it takes to squash a host of destructive behaviors.

Good Hike, Good Dog

Treat your dog to a day in the sun, and you'll appreciate the beauty of it long after you've returned home.

A well-exercised dog is eager to please and more easily trained. Tired and content, he or she will have little energy for begging and barking and being underfoot. Finally, dogs who indulge all their senses on nature's bounty have less of an appetite for the menu at home: the well-oiled baseball glove, those totally kickin' boots, your orthodontic retainer . . .

All I Really Need . . .

If your dog had the words to tell you everything that means anything to him in this world, he (or she!) wouldn't need many:

Alpha

Your dog's world already revolves around you. Expand his orbit to include adventures together outdoors, and the bond between Alpha and animal can grow even stronger. Imagine the effect that would have on your dog's training.

Exercise

Even with four legs to stand on, every extra pound weighs heavily on your dog's health. In breeds prone to joint or heart problems, weight issues or obesity are more dangerous still.

Head for the hills (at your dog's pace) to shed unwanted pounds and keep your friend fit.

Food

Chow, wow, wow. Your dog never misses a meal. But a healthy diet must include food for thought as well.

The sights, smells, sounds, and experiences of the trail nourish your dog's gray matter in ways that kibble can't.

Veterinarians, trainers, owners, and dogs unanimously agree that loved, nourished, well-exercised dogs are healthier, happier, and better behaved. Good hikes make good dogs.

Kids, dogs, and the pack as a whole agree that good hikes are made great with the addition of everybody's best friend.

CHAPTER 3

Some Dogs Are Mountain Goats
— Others Just Enjoy a Good Hike !—

Before you hit the trail, you have to ask yourself, "Just what kind of animal do we have here?" As Alpha, it's your responsibility to know your dog's unique abilities and limitations. Consider stamina, health, and physical build carefully before hiking off in the wrong direction.

Circle the Traits that Describe Your Dog

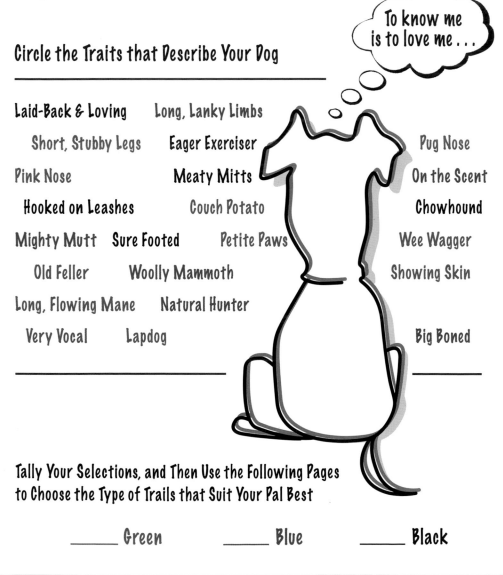

To know me is to love me . . .

Laid-Back & Loving   Long, Lanky Limbs

Short, Stubby Legs   Eager Exerciser   Pug Nose

Pink Nose   Meaty Mitts   On the Scent

Hooked on Leashes   Couch Potato   Chowhound

Mighty Mutt   Sure Footed   Petite Paws   Wee Wagger

Old Feller   Woolly Mammoth   Showing Skin

Long, Flowing Mane   Natural Hunter

Very Vocal   Lapdog   Big Boned

Tally Your Selections, and Then Use the Following Pages to Choose the Type of Trails that Suit Your Pal Best

_____ Green   _____ Blue   _____ Black

If Your Dog Is Looking Green

COUCH POTATO

If the traits that describe your dog are primarily green, chances are that he or she will prefer a gentler hike or need special consideration along the way.

LAPDOG The dog that prefers warming laps to running laps obviously will prefer shorter hikes with frequent breaks.

PUG NOSE The same goes for the pug-nosed pooch. Boxers, bulldogs, Pekingese, and pugs, for example, have flatter snouts that make breathing and self-cooling much more difficult.

Technically referred to as brachycephalic, these broad-skulled, short-nosed dogs are especially vulnerable to the dangers of heat stroke. Protect yours by setting a slow pace and taking frequent stops.

WEE WAGGER Starting out with a pup? Introduce her to hiking on soft, short nature trails close to home. For dogs younger than 12–14 months, long, rigorous hikes can damage still-growing joints and bones.

Your dog would climb mountains to please you, even if it wasn't so much fun. Just make sure that you don't bite off more than your dog can chew.

Less active dogs should start slow—working their way up from the evening stroll to brisk walks and greater distances before doing any serious hiking.

To avoid injury and maximize the fun, dogs and humans alike need to be well exercised and in good physical condition before bagging the summit.

OLD FELLER Older dogs also appreciate some babying to accommodate their senior stamina, achy joints, and other health conditions that can come with age. Give the old guy every advantage. If arthritis slows your pack from the get-go, invest in a lightweight ramp that allows your dog easy access to the car, or stick to easy paths close to home.

Short, interesting hikes with frequent rests beat staying home alone any day.

SHORT, STUBBY LEGS

Short legs work harder to keep up with the pack, and dainty paws will find steep or rocky paths a challenge at any pace. Be prepared with a Plan B should your pup poop out before you do. A backpack-style pet carrier may be a worthwhile accessory for your smallest hikers.

Petite Paws

SHOWING SKIN Can you see skin through your dog's fur/hair? Dogs with thin coats and light-colored hair are more sensitive to the sun, as are breeds with a pink or dappled nose. **PINK NOSE** Before you head out, ask your veterinarian to suggest the best ways to protect your dog from sunburn. Shoot for morning hikes to avoid some of the heat and sun, and take frequent water breaks in the shade.

Remember your manners. If your young pup hasn't mastered basic obedience commands and social skills, you're likely to run into trouble on the trail.

Training outdoors, with all its natural distractions, is a must. Sidewalk encounters and regular doggy play dates (on and off her own turf) also prepare your pet for peacefully crossing paths with others.

If your dog is accustomed to voicing her excitement, remember that backcountry barking disturbs hikers and wildlife alike. Teach your pal to bark on command, so she'll also understand a firm "No barking" on the trail.

LONG, FLOWING MANE

Perhaps your dog wears her hair long and loose. As you praise your pal for her super stamina and marvelous trail manners, check her hair carefully for burrs, debris, and the well-hidden tick. Such souvenirs you can do without!

THE BASENJI IS THE ONLY DOG BREED THAT CAN'T BARK.

Very Vocal
Very Vocal

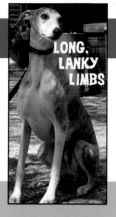

LONG, LANKY LIMBS

If daring and dexterity are qualities exemplified in your particular pooch, you may find that your dog enjoys rock hopping and bouldering as much as you. Just make sure to look before he leaps. Loose rocks, mossy crossings, and natural crevices can twist and trap slender legs and paws.

Trails carpeted with loose, uneven rock (called scree) can be tough on your dog's dogs, so check toes and footpads often, and watch your dog for limping or discomfort.

Dogs will often soldier on when they should be taking R & R. If necessary, make the command decision to fall back and safeguard your heroic troops.

True-blue Companions

True-blue companions can go the extra mile with their longer legs; larger, more stable paws; and a coat that provides natural sun protection.

Although hardy, these hardworking hounds, like all dogs, need plenty of water when on the go. Shorter muzzles (less effective at cooling) and bushy, black coats may mean your thirsty dog will need even more.

BIG BONED It's the loving dog owner who honestly evaluates her beloved, big-boned beauty. How much of your dog's girth is macho muscle, and how much is love handles? Dogs carrying extra body fat will get a more intense, cardio workout. Watch for signs that she's had enough.

WOOLLY MAMMOTH

A dog's coat may also dictate what type of hiking suits him best.

Is your dog likely to be overdressed? Fido's fur can help protect him from the sun's burning rays, but it can also trap dangerous amounts of body heat. Carry extra water, and start your hikes early in the day, when temperatures are cooler.

When you return home, don't forget to check all that fur for ticks and trail trash.

Under normal conditions, hiking dogs need at least two to three times as much water as they ordinarily drink at home. Crank up the heat and humidity, or the difficulty of terrain, and your dog will need even more. To avoid coming up short, it's smart to turn back when half of your water supply is gone.

NATURAL HUNTER Breeds that are known as hunters, herders, or all-around workhorses are apt to relish the challenge of rough terrain and rambling trails.

ON THE SCENT Scent trails and wildlife sightings can be particularly stimulating for these eager companions, so make sure that you have a firm grip on the leash at all times. You and your dog are, after all, guests in nature. Good manners dictate that you refrain from running wild and terrorizing your hosts.

The bigger the beast, the more it takes to control his enthusiasm for life.

MIGHTY MUTT Obedience training and real-life experience are the only ways to truly equip yourself to deal with this force of nature. There's no way around it—literally—since you're guaranteed to meet up with others (and their dogs) on skinny paths and trails.

If you use a training collar when working with your pet, you're not alone. When used correctly, training collars that tighten around a dog's neck, chest, or shoulders provide your dog with feedback that reinforces proper behavior.

When gearing up for a hike, however, it's best to leave this particular training tool at home. Such collars present a choking hazard should your pet escape and become entangled in the underbrush, or need to be reeled in to safety.

A simple, well-fitted body harness can provide adequate control while safeguarding your pet against neck strain and injury.

YOUR DOG SHOULD ALWAYS WEAR A SNUG NECK COLLAR WITH RABIES TAG, LICENSE, AND ID ATTACHED.

LAID-BACK & LOVING

Dogs who love exercise can sometimes overdo it. Rest, regular snacks, and plenty of water will keep your hiker in good health.

If Our Survey Paints Your Dog Black

If your dog is faster than a speeding Frisbee and able to leap tall staircases in a single bound, you may find it tough to keep up with your heroic companion on the trail.

Just don't let that kind of power get away from you.

HOOKED ON LEASHES Always keep a leash on your dog, not only for his safety but also that of the hikers and wildlife around you. Nothing brings out your dog's wild side like the wilderness.

To some extent, a dog's endurance on the trail increases with the length of her nose.

Unlike you, dogs can't work up a nice, cooling sweat when they're hot. Instead, they utilize the evaporative cooling capacity provided by the mouth and tongue—they pant. Breeds with longer snouts and tongues make better panters because there's more saliva-slicked surface to increase evaporation. Plus, long, straight nasal passages mean that the breathing comes easier as well. Cool!

MEATY MITTS

SURE FOOTED Sturdy, well-conditioned dogs often make perfect pack mules. Many are fully willing and able to carry some or all of their food and water supply on the trail. Just make sure that you don't saddle your pet with this new responsibility out of the blue.

Like all smart hikers, your dog should break in new gear long before reaching the trailhead. Begin with an empty pack around the house before moving on to a trial run through the neighborhood. Give your dog time to get comfortable with the experience, or *you* may end up carrying the dog pack on the trail.

For every 1,000 feet of elevation gain, plan an extra mile round-trip when evaluating a trail's level of difficulty.

CHOWHOUND Is your large dog a marvel of bone and muscle or just a whole lot of hug?

When a dog is packing extra pounds, any exercise weighs more heavily on his heart, muscles, and joints. Hiking takes your dog farther and farther away from the relief of a comfy chair or medical attention. So before you hook up with fellow hikers, ask the vet if your dog is up to the challenge.

EAGER EXERCISER Walk your energetic dog whenever you can, but never let your dog walk you.

Whether you're headed up a trail or around the block, your dog should respect your Alpha-ness and never pull at the end of his leash. On a narrow hiking trail, it could mean the difference between gazing into a peaceful valley and being dragged down into it.

Hardworking, fun loving, well behaved—your dog will win all sorts of praise from fellow hikers. Take care, however, if your dog is inclined to show his unreserved gratitude in return. Not everyone welcomes the attention of a dog that's too friendly.

Since the very first wolves banded together to ensure their survival, every dog born is hard-wired for family.

As your dog travels with his pack through the wild, that instinctive loyalty can make confrontations with other dogs unpredictable.

Snap on a leash, and you automatically create boundaries for your dog— territory he actually may feel he needs to defend.

If your dog tenses as others approach on the trail, step aside, shorten the slack in his leash, and reassure him with cheerful praise.

P. S. Don't count on every dog to be well trained, nor every owner to be considerate and prepared. Look out for your own and trouble is less likely to come looking for you.

Obviously, Dogs are Colorful Characters

Every member of the pack comes with his or her own unique mix of abilities and challenges—all of which will accompany you on the trail.

As Alpha, it's your responsibility to consider the special needs of your dog. Consult your veterinarian. Watch your dog closely, and trust your instincts.

With a little planning, no dog has to miss out on the fun of a family hike.

Would you believe that the poodle's poof was originally styled to make him a better hunter? This water retriever was clipped close to the body to minimize drag in the water and snags in the underbrush. Her curls were left long elsewhere to protect vital areas from the elements. Brightly colored bows adorned the ears to help a hunter distinguish his swimmer from the pack.

The name poodle *comes from the German word* pudeln, *which means "to paddle or splash."*

According to Search & Rescue Dogs of Colorado, a trained search dog can cover as much ground as 30 humans. SARDOC teams typically train 2–3 years, 300–500 hours per year, to become qualified.

After nine months and 2,167 miles, Bill Irwin became the first blind person to hike the entire length of the Appalachian Trail. Leading the way was his German shepherd guide dog, Orient, without whom he may have never reached his goal.

CHAPTER 4

RALLY THE PACK

Plan to Have an Awesome Adventure

Not every expedition will lead your pack far from home. But every hike and hiker can benefit from the confidence that comes with being prepared for just about anything. A bit of planning now will put you in good shape for the countless good times ahead.

You Never Hike the Same Trail Twice

Every hike presents its own unique challenges and rewards, even along trails that you've been traveling for years.

No, never this particular trail at this hour, this time of year . . . not after 3 days of rain, on a full stomach, with a wind from the south . . .

Pooch Packing List

- ☐ 6-foot leash
- ☐ dog harness
- ☐ webbed or leather collar
- ☐ ID tags: local contact info
- ☐ seat restraint or crate
- ☐ favorite blanket and a toy
- ☐ the usual chow, treats
- ☐ drinking water
- ☐ food & water bowls
- ☐ poop bags
- ☐ vaccination records
- ☐ emergency numbers
- ☐ first-aid kit
- ☐ emergency whistle
- ☐ old towels

Weather fronts move in, winds shift, buds sprout, and mature offspring set out on their own. The only thing certain from one excursion to the next is change.

Find out what you're getting into before packing up and heading out. Weather, trail conditions, elevation, and terrain will affect the quality of your outdoor experience.

Trade Out the Training Collar

Fussing with your dog over the proper execution of heel is no vacation for either of you, and it can be intrusive to others' enjoyment of an otherwise peaceful trail.

Adjusting your dog's harness requires the "try, try again" approach. Worn too tightly or loosely, a harness can pinch and rub, making you both miserable.

If you need any more reason to leave the fancy collars at home, it's this: your dog's safety.

Hiking dogs are excited dogs, and excited dogs (even well-trained ones) pull. In this situation, a neck collar puts enormous strain on your dog's anatomy and breathing. Training collars, most of which tighten at the neck by design, clamp down on your partner's excitement even more.

Now consider the entirely possible scenario in which you need to quickly pull your dog to safety, or your dog escapes and becomes tangled in thick brush. Let's just say that there's a reason so many training collars are referred to as choke chains.

A safer choice for the strong and rambunctious (and the mild mannered as well) is a simple, close-fitting harness. Anything new should be broken in before you hit the trail to make sure it doesn't rub your pet the wrong way.

Before you hook up and head out, check your dog's harness and leash for worn, weak spots or burrs hanging around from your last hike.

Better yet, make it a habit to clean your dog's gear regularly. It will last longer and be less likely to irritate his skin.

Go Long
Retractable leads and designer dog leashes are fine for a walk in the park, but the ideal hiking leash—a simple, sturdy, 6-foot standard—will make the hike safer and more enjoyable for both of you.

Bring the Bling!

A looped ring will secure your dog's tags better than the typical S-hook.

The classic neck collar aglitter with ID and vaccination tags complements any dog's hiking ensemble. Keep the contact information on those tags current, and consider adding a cell phone number so that lost dogs can reach you on the trail.

When you're hiking far from home, a set of easy-to-read, temporary tags can identify the local hotel or residence where you're staying.

Of the millions of dogs lost each year, few are ever reunited with their families. Up-to-date, easy-to-read tags are a lost dog's most effective means of enlisting help and finding his way home. Today, more and more families choose to microchip their pet as well. In this affordable procedure, a tiny computer chip encoded with an owner's contact information is inserted just beneath the dog's skin. Ask your veterinarian or local animal shelter about this program.

Keep a favorite photo of your pet in your wallet. If your dog becomes lost, it will help others assist in your search.

First Impressions Count

What a dog wears on the trail says a lot about who he or she is. A fresh, colorful collar, bandanna, or leash says, "I'm someone's pet," and "you're gonna love me!" That can be a welcomed introduction for the hiker startled by your dog's sudden appearance around the bend.

A fetching bandana softens a girl's look. Soak it in water, and it can also help keep a hot dog cool.

To Buy or Not to Buy

These days, you almost need a map to navigate your way through the mountains of clever products designed for the hiking hound. Rest assured that, with a few exceptions, your dog will have just as much fun without a full complement of gear.

In fact, much of what we buy for our dogs is stuff designed to appeal to us humans. That's what makes shopping for pets so much fun.

Just remember that the goodies you carry into the woods must come back out. If fancy accessories become an annoyance or burden for your dog, you'll be the one to pack them out.

Dog booties are meant to protect paws over hostile terrain like super-hot pavement and jagged debris. On the typical day hike, booties simply aren't necessary. In fact, the wrong pair can compromise your dog's footing and collect pebbles and dirt.

If you just have to have 'em, keep them in your first-aid kit for protecting injured paws. A pair of baby socks and duct tape can serve that purpose, as well.

To Buy

Fresh drinking water being so crucial on every hike, it's a safe bet that a collapsible water dish for your friend will be one of your favorite hiking accessories. No water wasted and no slobber shared.

A FRESH "DOGGIE BAG" WITH SIDES ROLLED DOWN CAN STAND IN FOR A FORGOTTEN WATER BOWL.

Pack It In, Pack It Out

Everything you and your pal bring to the party – not just the banana peels and soda cans and candy wrappers –but anything you would not want to see or smell or step in – should be bagged, carried out, and disposed of properly (and we do mean doo-doo).

Hiking's Hard Work

It's not every dog that can herd sheep, guide the blind, or detect items smuggled in a locked suitcase.

Most, however, will doggedly work overtime for added affection and praise. On the trail, that job may be as simple as boldly leading her people into the unknown. The sturdy dog can take on weightier responsibilities, such as carrying her own water and treats. Being "employed" is its own reward for your socially driven pack animal.

Of course, not every body is cut out for this kind of work. Such specialized labor requires fitness, training, and practice at home and on the trail.

When choosing a dog pack, prepare to be picky. The size and style that best fits your dog is one that:

- balances the weight of the pack on your dog's shoulders, not mid-back
- allows free movement of your dog's legs
- positions filled saddlebags low on the torso for better balance and less bounce
- holds snug to the body, with buckles and straps positioned to minimize friction
- uses lightweight, breathable, or mesh fabrics to help your canine keep his cool

To avoid injury and fatigue, never ask a dog to carry more than 10% of his own body weight. Have a heart, and carry your own beef jerky as well.

Getting in Gear for the Hike

Being accustomed to walking about in his birthday suit, your free-spirited dog will need a chance to get comfortable with his new hiking gear.

Pack smart. Frozen water bottles of equal size can help balance saddlebags and keep your dog cool.

Start slowly with an empty pack around the house. Crumpled grocery bags and a tin of breath mints make a good first haul due to the rattling sound effects they provide. Later, add a water bottle on each side and stroll the neighborhood. Lead him up and down stairs and over the occasional ditch so he learns to adjust for shifting cargo.

Now Walk a Mile in Your Shoes

You evaluated your dog's personal fitness for the hike pages ago. You know her strengths, her weaknesses, and how to equip her for success.

No matter how well you prepare for your dog's outdoor adventures, however, she's going to be miserable if you are. Getting yourself into good shape for the trail, physically and mentally, is every bit as important as preparing your dog.

Prepare to Have Fun

With the possible exception of the leash and ID tags, your pre-hike checklist should look a lot like the one for your dog.

Pack more than enough water, plenty of snacks, and extra clothes and towels in your car. Wear sunscreen. Carry bug spray. Grab your leash, and go!

> Resist the temptation to chow down before a hike. Small meals throughout the day are best for hikers of all species. Just make sure that "snackers" stop panting first.

Packing People

- ☐ good hiking shoes and comfortable socks for all but the gentlest path; key for slippery stream crossings, uneven paths, and steep climbs. (Plus, you won't be tempted to bypass a muddy trail if you're wearing shoes devoted to the job.)

- ☐ water, water, water — roughly 16 ounces of water per hiker, per hour; more in hot and humid conditions. DON'T wait until you're thirsty to drink. Keep a full cooler in the car for the end-of-trail cooldown.

- ☐ dress in layers — Even day hikers need to change with the weather. Pack a layer for wet or windy conditions.

- ☐ emergency whistle — Every hiker should be packing one; invaluable for reuniting separated pack members and shooing curious wildlife.

- ☐ sunscreen, a hat, and bug repellent

- ☐ superhuman trail snacks — These are portable, minimally messy, and healthy. Try grapes, raisins, chocolate, nuts, or fruit. NEVER SHARE with your pet, as all of these can be toxic to your dog.

- ☐ camera — You will be leaving every flower, every rock, leaf, and stick in its place for the next lucky hiker to enjoy.

Rx for Rex

If your dog's middle name is Trouble (or Cuddles or Thor or . . .), you'll want to be prepared for any scrapes he may wag his way into. Fortunately, a well-stocked, standard first-aid kit can doctor both man and beast. There are a few items that are particularly helpful when traveling and hiking with pets.

MOST DOGS HAVE A VERY HIGH TOLERANCE FOR PAIN. WATCH YOUR PAL CAREFULLY FOR SIGNS OF DISTRESS.

Add to First-aid Kit

☐ eye wash — because where the nose goes . . .

☐ hydrogen peroxide — to clean wounds and induce vomiting (use 1-2 Tbsp.)

☐ *styptic powder + cotton swabs — to clot blood from a torn or broken toenail

☐ alcohol wipes — to disinfect small wounds

☐ comb or brush

☐ muzzle — because injury makes pets unpredictable

☐ *vet wrap + sterile gauze pads — for wounds and wrapping limbs

☐ old beach towel — a stretcher for an injured dog, warmth for a pet in shock, or a rag for wet paws

☐ baby socks or dog booties — to cover bandaged paws

☐ duct tape

☐ emergency vet number and vaccination records

☐ Fido's photo — in case your pet is lost

*Items available from your veterinarian and most pet supply stores.

CHAPTER 5

Go, Dog, Go

> Ohhhh, yeah!
> Goin' to Grandmaaaa's!
> No? OO! OO! The bank!

Road-tripping with the Family

What is it about best friends and road trips that hold such promise? The journey? The destination? The fire hydrants whipping by?

Sure, your pal considers practically any car ride kibbles and gravy. But if you want to see him really drool, crack the windows and head for the hills. Or the waterfront. Or your nearest state or national park. Whether you pick up your trail from the community greenbelt or 100 miles down the road, hiking with your dog is the only way to go.

STOP Don't even back out of the driveway without making sure that your dog's rabies and other vaccinations, as well as protection against heartworms, fleas, and ticks, are up-to-date. Your dog will be mixing with a wild crowd out there, and the best protection is prevention.

Even if you're merely headed down the road to a favorite trail, always stuff a sack with your dog in mind—beginning with lots of water and an appropriate collar and leash (see pages 14 and 19 for more details).

Avoiding Bumps in the Road

Beyond the drippy nose prints, past the constant flicker of sun and shade and trees, your dog's stomach is being taken for a ride.

Like their owners, dogs can get carsick watching the world whip by.

A comfortably snug, canine harness/seat belt can keep your dog's window-hopping to a minimum. If your dog travels in a secured crate, a thin sheet or pillowcase can block out the dizzying view.

SAVE LONGER ROAD TRIPS FOR MILDER MONTHS—FOR KINDER TEMPERATURES IN YOUR CAR AND ON THE TRAIL.

Unless your vet recommends otherwise, never give your pet tranquilizers for the road. They may not sit well in your dog's stomach and will make him wobbly on the trail.

Press your nose to the window long enough, and you'll see all kinds of unsafe drivers on the road—including some who dart window to window monitoring traffic, and pull up to every stoplight panting and drooling. Regardless of his size or the depth of his intelligence, a dog has no business being in the driver's seat. Statistics show that driver distraction accounts for more accidents than any other issue.

Sadly, nearly 98% of pets on the go are not properly restrained. An untethered dog can easily become a high-speed projectile in a crash.

Allowing your dog to ride shotgun, belted in or not, also puts your pet at risk because even a minor fender bender can trigger an air bag to deploy.

Your dog's driving enthusiasm should always take a backseat to his safety.

In a 35-mile-per-hour collision, an unrestrained, 60-pound dog can hit the windshield with 2,700 pounds of force. *

Nothing says freedom like the image of a dog with his head out the car window, ears flying. But, oh, the price of freedom!

Your pet is just begging for bugs and road dirt in the eyes, up the nose, between the teeth, and down the hatch. Half in, half out is certainly no place for your pooch in a crash. This precarious perch can even push air into a dog's lungs with enough force to injure fragile tissue. It's better to crack the window just a bit, and leave the flying to the birds.

*Bark Buckle UP, "Be Smart Ride Safe." (barkbuckleup.com)

Sit, Stand, Down—Stay

The safest, coziest ride for your pal depends on the size of your dog and your car, as well as personal preference.

An effective restraint needn't tie your dog down. In fact, most options allow freedom of movement for maximum comfort and even sightseeing, while ensuring that your dog will stay put in an emergency.

Padded perches give small dogs a better view, heart-hugging harnesses are available for dogs of all sizes, and first-class crates can be tethered into the back of a van, wagon, or SUV.

In no time, most dogs actually appreciate the familiarity and security of this new car-ride routine. After all, who wants to be seen careening across the leather or plunging nose-first into the floorboards?

Woof! That's gotta hurt!

Does Your Dog's Restraint Fit You?

Before you buy, match the restraint's recommended weight limits to your particular pooch, and make sure that it is compatible with the family car. In the end, the right choice will probably be the one that best suits the humans in the pack. The easier it is to buckle in, the more likely you'll use it every time.

Remember that a pet restraint is important to the safety of everyone in your car.

A Great Crate Is:

- big enough for your dog to stand up and turn around comfortably

- located for maximum ventilation (without luggage and pillows piled on all sides)

- anchored so that it can't tip or slide

Are We There Yet?

Ironically, the dog that puts down roots in the middle of your bed each night rarely sits quietly in the car for long.

When your plans begin with a significant amount of car travel, remember to consider your companion's needs. Pack distractions—a squeak toy, a favorite chew, or ice cubes for munching—to take some of the bite out of boredom. Be prepared to make pit stops. Larger, active dogs need more frequent stops to stretch their legs and to express their enthusiasm for the adventures ahead.

OPEN CAR DOORS AND WINDOWS WIDE AFTER BOTH LONG HIKES AND SHORT PIT STOPS. HOT SEATS AND BELT BUCKLES CAN BURN. HAVE YOUR DOG WAIT IN THE SHADE, NOT ON HOT PAVEMENT.

Dogs are creatures of habit, and too many changes in routine can create stress and unpleasant problems, the likes of which you won't enjoy cleaning up in your car or on the trail.

Familiar comforts such as a favorite blanket, and especially your dog's plain old everyday dog food and treats, will mean happier trails for all.

i'm hungry!

Lap It Up

Staying hydrated is important for everyone in the car, even before the hard work of hiking begins. Pack more drinking water than you think is necessary, along with a stash of ice cubes and a dog dish for easy, in-transit hydration.

On longer drives, stop regularly and often. Remember to hook your dog's leash before opening any doors. Even a well-behaved dog may jump out into traffic when motivated by an urgent need to pee.

Heading out early? Wait to feed your dog until you've reached your destination. Otherwise, you run the risk of seeing her breakfast twice.

CHAPTER 6

Put Your Best Paw Forward

Come!
Sit!
Stay!
Down!
No Bark!

Civility's Place in the Wilderness

Remember the last time that you jumped on a total stranger or pushed past the couple ahead of you in line? For the sake of argument, let's just assume that your answer is, "NO!"

Rude behavior is no more acceptable from your dog. In fact, a reckless pooch on the trail can pose a real threat to hikers' safety—on narrow trails, on rocky terrain, or in unexpected confrontations.

Yes, dogs will be dogs. But you can insist that yours be on his best behavior at all times and respond to basic training commands.

More Dogs – More Muscle

Crossing paths with hiking hounds is a given. How your own pet will respond is not. Take control of the situation by passing the leash to the strongest member of the pack. In the end, it is the humans' job to maintain control in any situation.

IF A DOGFIGHT BREAKS OUT, BACK AWAY AND THROW WATER ON THE DOGS IF POSSIBLE. HUMAN SAFETY TAKES PRIORITY.

One Person, One Leash, One Dog

If you happen to be blessed with a large and exuberant pack, spread the enthusiasm among your Alphas (of the human variety). One person, one leash, one dog is the safest, most enjoyable way to travel, especially when paths turn tricky and when you meet traffic from the opposite direction.

Many of the policies governing your backcountry treks are as official as the National Park Service. Others carry the weight of simple good manners and common sense. Together, these guidelines can help you avoid pileups and navigate potholes on the trail.

Stick to the Trail

Don't let enthusiasm incite you to take shortcuts or break out of line on the trail. Wayward hikers can flatten fragile plant life, widen the trail, and contribute to trail erosion.

A trail is only as wide as it needs to be. Encourage your group to travel single file to minimize your impact on the natural landscape. If some self-appointed trailblazer has left you with an alternate route, choose the path *most* taken. Encourage others to do the same, and you'll give nature a chance to re-carpet where less-considerate visitors have tracked in the mud.

The National Park Service is charged with safeguarding irreplaceable natural resources and wildlife. However, it's a responsibility that we all share. Do your part by knowing and respecting park regulations wherever you hike.

HOOK UP WITH MORE INFORMATION ON OUR NATIONAL PARKS AT NPS.GOV.

Most state and federal public lands have very specific regulations regarding hiking hounds; where allowed, dogs must be restrained at all times on a leash no longer than 6 feet.

Always check the rules for your destination before you leave home.

"BUT WHY?" "Why keep my well-behaved, fully trained, completely harmless, beloved family pet on leash?"

Natural Instinct — Face it: your dog's ancestors were a pack of wolves; all dogs are programmed for the chase.

The Natural Order of Things — Most wildlife perceives a loose dog in one of two ways: as a threat or a meal.

Human Nature — A dog that runs free will eventually cross paths with a hiker who considers your dog's freedom a nuisance, a menace, or just plain unacceptable.

Give him a good scare, and that hiker may raise a ruckus with management— a consequence that can jeopardize our right to hike with pets at all.

Secure Fido's Freedoms with a Leash

Travel as a Pack

Your dog's earliest ancestors understood the drawbacks to being a lone wolf. As the saying goes, "There's safety in numbers."

Never hike alone, and always share your itinerary with those at home.

If switchbacks, dense forest, and forks in the trail threaten to divide the pack, adjust your speed so your people are close at hand.

Give 'em Some Leash

Of course, you'll also want to give your trail mates room to enjoy the still, clean air—unspoiled by the clouds of dust kicking up at your feet.

Following at a safe distance puts you out of range when the random branch whips back in a hiker's wake. A buffer between hikers will also quiet your progress, increasing your odds of sighting timid wildlife.

While you're at it, give your dog some room. She'll appreciate the 6 feet of freedom that a good hiking leash provides. You'll appreciate that she's not underfoot.

Turn Back Now and Again

There's no better way to appreciate the magnitude of your hiking accomplishments than to turn back occasionally to see where you've been.

In addition to enjoying the view, you'll become familiar with the trail from every angle. The added confidence and security of seeing familiar natural landmarks on your way home is well worth a break in momentum.

Well-established trails are often marked with some type of trail blaze (above and below), post, or cairn (left). Memorizing unique natural landmarks can also help you navigate adventures with confidence.

Share the Love

As peaceful and private as your wilderness experience can be, you will inevitably cross paths with a variety of nature enthusiasts. So who has the right of way?

Most often, your own good manners will show the way. When in doubt, it's generally best to yield to the larger, more rapidly moving mass.

Be prepared to make room on the trail for a passing horse and rider, a string of mountain bikes, or the lone jogger.

Other hikers with dogs can also present an impasse. On leash in an unfamiliar environment, some dogs may behave aggressively, protecting their territory as well as their pack.

Don't assume that your sweetheart will be all cuddles and wags. Step aside and let the other party pass, keeping your dog close in a quiet, nonnegotiable "Sit!"

"If a Dog Poops in the Woods..."

Ironically, some of the same folks who meticulously remove their pet's mess from the neighbor's yard often leave his poop where it's put on the trail.

"... Does It Still Stink?"

Does it really matter if you clean up after your pet when you're out in the wilderness?

Ask yourself that question after you make an unfortunate misstep, or your dog decides to roll in another dog's mess.

Ask the locals. The scent message left behind by your dog's doings can be threatening to timid wildlife wary of becoming prey. It can aggravate others who have claimed the territory as their own. Your dog's pile may even introduce harmful nutrients, foreign bacteria, and viruses into a fragile ecosystem.

So bag that bad boy and carry it out.

Watch Your Step

With four paws and a low center of gravity, most dogs can handle any twist in the trail. You, however, may find that loose rock and dry, sandy descents have a way of pulling your feet out from under you.

Sidestepping down steep grades can provide you with more traction, especially when you're wearing sturdy-soled shoes. Keep some slack in your dog's leash so that sudden movements won't jerk you off balance.

It's All about the Journey

One of the greatest things about hiking with dogs is that they compel you to slow down and appreciate the countless small wonders in nature.

A wise old dog once said, "Life is about the journey, not the destination." Then he returned to smelling the same bush five minutes more.

Sometimes, however, your pal's appreciation of every last smell slows the hike to a crawl. Or perhaps your dog's drive to explore is so strong that he drags you recklessly up the trail. Either way, you may find yourself wondering if you're actually having fun.

Hang in there. The more ground you cover, the more relaxed and cooperative your dog will become. As hiking becomes a more regular part of his life, he'll be less desperate to drink it all in at once.

For now, take a deep, deep breath of clean air, forget about where you're going, and enjoy the sights along the way.

Stopping for lunch? Let your dog stop panting before you offer food, and then let his stomach settle before resuming the hike.

Keep America Beautiful

The most important thing you can carry up the trail is a healthy respect for both the power and the fragility of nature.

Every hiker shares the responsibility of safeguarding the health and beauty of the living treasure around us. So while you're setting your sights on the summit, a favorite waterfall, or shaded picnic site, make it your goal to "Leave No Trace" of your expedition along the way.

Every rock, fern, and feather is part of the natural beauty you came so far to see. Resist the temptation to pocket "just one" pebble or pinecone, and you help ensure that the hike will be just as rewarding for the next lucky dog to come along.

Collect memories, not mementos.

FOR INFORMATION ON LOW-IMPACT HIKING AND CAMPING, CHECK OUT LNT.ORG.

CHAPTER 7

TRAITS OF A TRAIL HOUND
— A Nose For Adventure —

Moments after her paws hit the ground, your dog knows more about the nature of the trail ahead than this book can begin to describe.

Common scents tell her the who, what, when, where, why, and how of the world around you with incredible detail.

- Animal, vegetable, or mineral?
- Male or female?
- Dominant or submissive?
- Healthy or ill?
- Headed this way or that?
- Friend or foe?
- What was for dinner?

Dogs can distinguish subtle chemical changes, such as those that can accompany illness, and have even detected cancers and imminent seizures in their humans.

A dog's sense of smell is thought to be as much as 10,000 times more powerful than our own. Trained scent dogs can potentially discriminate as many as 1,000,000 unique odors and even detect familiar scents masked by the fog of an angry skunk.

Follow that nose, and you're likely to discover a host of visual clues to back your witness's remarkably detailed account of the day's news.

THE NASAL MEMBRANES LINING A DOG'S NOSE, IF LAID FLAT, COULD EXCEED THE SIZE OF THE DOG ITSELF (A SMALL DOG'S NOSE IS PROPORTIONALLY STUFFED)!*

*Bruce Fogle, *The Dog's Mind: Understanding Your Dog's Behavior* (New York: Howell Book House, 1992).

Scent Receptors

Human Nose
~5-10 million

Small Dog Nose
~125 million

Medium Nose
~145 million

Large Nose
~220-plus million

Genetics also dictate the number of scent receptors in a dog's nose. Not all big noses are equally super sniffers.

How Our Scents Abilities Compare

Inside every nose, moist skin is populated with nerve endings that detect scent molecules in the air.

Now consider that a dog's nose is all but stuffed with this tissue. Fold after sticky fold of sensitive, nerve-packed tissue collects, traps, and processes a world of information.

Obviously, the difference between your nose and your dog's is big, and a bigger nose (snout included) equals more nerves.

Tuning in to Smell-o-vision

In a whiff, the volumes of information collected by your dog are distilled into a rich, detailed scenario. See, your dog not only has a bigger beak than you, but she also has a much larger, more developed smell center in her brain to interpret this never-ending flow of input.

This sensory network even includes a separate channel for interpreting specific scent messages called pheromones. Located above the roof of the mouth, this extra olfactory organ uses different scent receptors to communicate with yet another region in the brain—one believed to govern sexual and social behavior. Impulses sent here may enhance a dog's ability to recognize specific animals and humans.

Further refinements in this path to enlightenment include the slits on the sides of a dog's nose. These ducts allow each moist exhale to churn the air, forcing even juicier scent molecules in with the next breath.

Some natural trackers, such as bloodhounds, work with their noses to the ground, inhaling a trail of clues/skin cells left by his quarry. Such dogs are referred to as trailing dogs.

Specially trained scent dogs are now leading field researchers in the study of wildlife populations, rare and endangered species, invasive plant life, snow leopards, cheetahs, and even whales. Their ability to detect the slightest differences among a host of competing odors makes them incredibly efficient at zeroing in on their subject. These dogs not only save biologists hours of work in the field, but they also save precious research dollars as well.

"Air-scent" dogs hold their heads high, scanning for a cone of concentrated scent molecules in the air.

The Smell of Leather

The next time you give your sweetheart an Eskimo kiss, take a moment to admire those remarkable dimples that make up the tip of his nose—his "nose leather."

All those moist bumps and crevices are designed to attract, grab, and dissolve scent molecules as your dog sniffs them in. Sometimes dogs lick their noses to speed the process along. Ask your dog to sit for a treat and see if he doesn't lick his nose to sample the anticipated treat.

Of course, not all noses are alike. In some breeds, the nose leather is spotted or pink and is even prone to sunburn. What's more, the grain of each dog's nose leather is entirely unique—just like the one-of-a-kind fingerprints belonging to you.

How Cool Is That Nose?

Even the flattest of dog noses is more sensitive than yours; pugs and pointers alike can put you on the trail of something big.

However, as the nose grows, so do its astounding abilities.

Because dogs can't sweat, they pant to beat the heat. All that unbridled tongue wagging lowers body temperature by speeding up evaporation in the mouth. As the saliva evaporates, it disperses body heat with it, just as perspiration does for you.

The coolest dog noses, then, are the bigger, longer ones accompanied by a sizable stretch of tongue. The greater the slobbery surface area exposed to evaporation, the cooler the hot dog.

Always be aware of your dog's cooling capacity when planning your hikes. Start early while the day is cool, and always seek shade when you stop for breaks.

CHAPTER 8

TRAITS OF A TRAIL HOUND
— Exceptional Ears —

If you can wiggle your ears at will, you are truly a rare breed of human. If your dog can do it, well, she's just your average, amazing dog.

Dogs have 20 muscles dedicated to the movement of their ears. Most can change the position and even the shape of their ears to capture and pinpoint distant sounds from all directions.

MOST DOGS CAN IDENTIFY FAMILY MEMBERS BY THEIR FOOTSTEPS OR THE SOUND OF THEIR CAR.

This keen ability to zero in also helps your dog filter out the sounds he most wants to hear. Think about it. Your stereo is thrumming, the TV is blaring, your sister is on the phone, and—pffft—the sound of a tuna can being opened brings your dog running.

Now Hear This

Dogs can hear sounds of pitch and frequency that your ears were never designed to hear. They can also detect sounds four times farther away. So when you see your hiking partner perk up for no apparent reason, be alert. You just might hear "it" for yourself farther down the trail.

Sometimes, dogs' ears play a part in the sense of smell as well. In many breeds, evolution (assisted by breeders) threw a pair of dangling ears into the works. These expert trackers have the luxury of investigating a concentrated cloud of scent messages stirred up by, and trapped within, a velvety curtain of ears.

Ear Types

The tough skin that makes up the ear is often referred to as leather. The size and visibility of the ear leather varies greatly among breeds.

Spotting the Best Listeners

While all dogs are blessed with supersonic hearing of one degree or another, you can easily spot those dogs specially equipped to be the best listeners of all.

Dogs with upright ears, often referred to as prick ears, employ a set of flexible radar dishes to track and funnel sound from all directions. The ear's size, and even its position on the head, can further enhance your dog's naturally brilliant sensitivity to sound.

How Many Ears Can a Dog Have?

The multitalented canine ear comes in so many sizes and shapes that breeders have come up with a slew of names to describe them. These are just a few of the ears you'll see walking out and about. Remember, a lot of our best friends are mixed breeds, so the shape and style, in general, are not an exact science.

- V-shaped
- Prick
- Triangular
- Button
- Candle Flame
- Tulip
- Rose
- High
- Low
- Close
- Wide
- Dropped
- Semi-dropped
- Heart
- Bat
- Flying

The list goes on . . .

Your dog's ears also speak volumes about how she's feeling: anxious, alert, humble, or fierce. The changing posture of those ears conveys meaning to others in her species and in her adopted pack.

TRAINED SERVICE DOGS ACT AS EARS FOR THE DEAF, ALERTING THEM TO SIGNALS FROM ALARM CLOCKS AND SMOKE ALARMS.

Who doesn't love the classic head tilt? This posture can be a response to new or unfamiliar sounds, or perhaps the utter brilliance of a beloved owner's words.

EARS ARE A FAVORITE HIDEOUT FOR TICKS, BURRS, AND BACTERIA. ALWAYS CHECK THEM AFTER A HIKE, AND HAVE YOUR VET DEMONSTRATE BASIC EAR CARE.

CHAPTER 9

TRAITS OF A TRAIL HOUND
— A Keen Eye —

Before the dog bowl, there was the bounty of nature. Kibble came in a multitude of shapes and sizes; all a dog had to do was find it.

Keen eyesight made it easier for early canines to spot their next meal, as well as avoid becoming a meal themselves. On the trail, those eyes can alert you to wild entertainment that you don't want to miss.

Your Dog Doesn't Miss Much

Camouflage is rarely enough to conceal an animal's movement from your dog. Dogs can spot an object in motion from as much as a half-mile away, and even recognize details such as familiar postures or gait.

The Bigger Picture

Wide-set eyes give dogs incredible peripheral vision. On many longer-nosed breeds, the eyes are practically perched on the sides of the face, stretching the field of vision even more.

Your field of vision is about 180 degrees; for some dog breeds, it's more like 240 degrees. Close vision, however, is not one of a dog's strengths.

If pressed for details on objects right under his nose, however, Spot could provide a sketchy description at best. Wide-set eyes can barely see what's right in front of them, literally. Large canine pupils, so beautifully designed for vision in low light, don't lend themselves to close focus either. That's why all dogs rely on their super smart senses of smell and taste to fill in details up close.

As a package, your friend with the fuzzy vision essentially sees more of what's going on than you.

A Dog's Eyes Shine at Night

Canine eyes are stellar at picking up movement and seeing in low light.

Like our eyes, dogs' eyes are equipped with light receptors called rods and cones. Rods see in low light; cones see color. In your dog's eyes, the rods rule—making night vision a natural skill.

Unlike human eyes, a dog's eyes (along with a host of nocturnally inclined mammals) are further equipped with an enlightening feature called the tapetum. This special membrane amplifies and reflects available light back to the retina—greatly enhancing your pet's ability to see after dark.

See for Yourself

Set out on an evening walk to catch this eyeball upgrade at work. Sweep the beam of a flashlight quickly across your dog's face to find the twinkle in his eyes.

Flash on the ruckus in a nearby tree, and you might encounter a raccoon's icy glare. Naturalists who track and study animals at night call this steady, eerie glow "eye shine."

Try it on yourself in the mirror at home. Your own eyes, being human, will not exhibit eye shine.

Ever wonder why a camera's flash registers only an empty, hypnotic stare from your dog, yet clearly captures the devilment in your sister's eyes?

In your dog, the camera is documenting eye shine: light bouncing off of reflective cells in your dog's eyes. Lacking this special feature, human eyes often appear red in photographs. That devilish flare is the illumination of blood-enriched retinas. Unlike eye shine, red eye is a phenomenon that exists only in low-light, flash photography. The effect is so instantaneous that it can be seen only by a camera's super-fast lens.

Dogs Have a Clear Advantage

To accommodate furious digging, dense underbrush, and harsh conditions, evolution 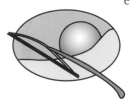 equipped the canine eye with a hidden, third eyelid called the nictitating membrane. These underappreciated eyelids reflexively blink to clear debris, as well as moisten and protect the eyes.

Never seen even a wink of your dog's wipers? That's a good thing. In most dogs, the nictitating membrane is noticeable only if it becomes inflamed.

Until recently, it was thought that a dog's world was black-and-white. Scientific and behavioral studies now suggest that dogs actually can differentiate a limited range of muted hues. Fewer cones (color receptors) mean that dogs' eyes aren't equipped to see the range of colors most humans do.

Old Yeller may see shades of blue and yellow, but his greens and reds are probably gray.

CHAPTER 10

TRACK LIKE THE EXPERTS

Follow That Dog!

Unless you're used to having the neighbors run and hide when you come knocking, you may be disappointed by the lack of a proper welcome from local wildlife.

Dogs, however, find such elusive behavior inviting and will eagerly begin gathering clues about the nature and whereabouts of these timid locals.

Follow your dog's nose, and you're sure to discover countless signs of life on the trail.

Scat

If your pal seems particularly engrossed in a trailside pile of poop, also known as feces or scat, you can be sure that he's catching up on the morning's news. That's your cue to gather some facts of your own.

Being nasally challenged by comparison, you will have to piece the story together with some sharp observation and common sense.

For example, a coyote's scat (see below) may indicate a diet of berries and seeds, or when prey is plentiful, scat may contain obvious fur and bone.

While your dog's powers of observation are superb, her judgment is abysmal when it comes to recognizing the dangers lurking in an innocent pile of poop.

Dogs are naturally drawn to investigate scat, but that doesn't mean you have to allow it. Listen to your own instincts (if it stinks, don't smell it) and cut her examination short.

Diseases can be transmitted to the dog with a taste for feces, and possibly even inhaled from the dried variety.

Dog poop left along the trail isn't scat; It's Inconsiderate.

Be a responsible hiker. Always carry bags and pick up after your pet.

Strict vegetarians, such as rabbits and deer, leave a very different pile of clues.

Skin and Bones

Many animals dine off a menu of small rodents and insects. Out of necessity, some even swallow their meal whole. So how do they digest all that fur and bones?

They don't. They regurgitate it, which is pretty much what it sounds like—gagging up your last meal. What a human diner might have left on the plate (better yet, on the cutting board) an owl will expel after digesting the good stuff.

Many bird and animal parents also regurgitate partly digested food to feed offspring that are too young to feed themselves.

These tangled wads of fur and bone, called owl pellets, can be found at the base of trees favored by roosting owls.

In need of a scent dog with wings, engineers in search of pipeline leaks have added a carrionlike odor to their gas lines and then followed vultures to the leaks—some as far as 40 miles away.

Few forest diners actually clean their plate after a meal. In fact, a successful predator's table scraps are the mainstay of many natural scavengers.

The turkey vulture, one of the few bird species with a sense of smell, is renowned for his scavenging skills. The vulture's unique beak can hone in on carrion far below the forest canopy before it even starts to rot. Vultures provide a valuable service to their ecosystem by ferreting out and picking clean abandoned carcasses that might otherwise breed disease.

Bark if You Love a Good Story

Mother Nature has some awesome stories to tell; a few can even be found etched into trees along the trail.

A pattern of gashes cut into tree bark may be the work of a bear marking territory.

In addition to sharp claws, these powerful paws are equipped with scent glands that make the bear's territorial claim perfectly clear to those who read with their nose.

Your guide's keen nose will recognize the scars on this tree (left) as an entirely different animal—an elk feeding on tender bark for a little winter nutrition.

Yet another bare spot, a buck rub, is created by a mature, male deer, which will mark territory by rubbing his antlers and scent against trees. Of course, he may also have been scratching an itch or polishing dried skin off his new headpiece to impress the girls.

The Hole Story

A perforated tree trunk such as this one can make you really appreciate the premade sandwich in your pack.

The pileated woodpecker spends the larger part of its day tapping this natural source of grub (insects, grubs, and tree sap). After hammering into the trunk, the bird uses its sticky, bristle-covered tongue to reach in and extract the hard-won treat.

Then again, not all holes are hammered. Close inspection may suggest a different culprit, one with a taste for trees. What other clues might you find if you were examining the handiwork of hungry insects?

Holes are Rarely Empty

In nature, many long-dead trees are actually full of life.

If your dog discovers droppings at the base of a rotting, hollow tree, you might find an active nesting or roosting site higher up.

Such trees, called snags, are also ideal homes for colonies of termites or ants.

Once occupied, that same snag makes an attractive snack shack for insect-loving birds, bears, and others.

Last Season's Look

Remember the last pair of blue jeans you inherited? Too tight, too short, or just plain out of style, hand-me-downs are a regular phenomenon for many animals as well.

For example, snakes grow throughout their lives, so they're continually outgrowing their skin. Snagging the old duds over rough bark and brambles to shuck their skin, snakes molt four to eight times a year or more.

Oddly enough, some part of nature is always waiting to snatch up just such a prize.

As a noun, the word *shed* can refer to the castoffs (down, skin, or antlers) that an animal has outgrown or no longer needs.

As impressive as a buck's antlers can be, you'd think that he spent years growing them. In fact, deer antlers mature in a matter of months, reaching full magnificence just in time to win favor with the ladies. In January, the antlers are shed, only to begin growing again early spring.

If snakes are always shedding and antlers are breaking off, why don't we see them littering the forest floor?

The furry sort shed, baby birds ditch their down . . . and another cozy layer is added to an animal's burrow or nest.

Eggshells split, skin sloughs off . . . and health food is added to the menu.

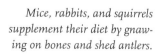

Mice, rabbits, and squirrels supplement their diet by gnawing on bones and shed antlers.

Food for Thought

Where there are snacks, there's usually a party, right?

If you're looking for signs of wildlife, you're apt to find some among the tender green shoots, seasonal fruits, and berries flanking the trail.

Broken branches, trampled brush, and nibbled vegetation generally mark popular picnic spots for a variety of grazing animals.

Water sources are also a daily gathering spot, so don't be surprised if your dog takes a special interest in the smells that abound here. What other clues might you sniff out in the brush?

Known as game trails, these animal-engineered paths often appear to be little more than a part combed into a lush stretch of vegetation.

Is there a dog on earth that doesn't turn a few circles in bed before hitting the hay?

That behavior is the remnant of an instinct that compels many wild animals to flatten a cozy, critter-free, camouflaged spot in the grass before bedding down for the night. Others think that circling may also orient the animal with its nose to the wind—which would carry the smell of approaching danger.

Busy Intersections

Your naturally perceptive trail guide may direct your attention to the occasional, pencil-thin path branching off the main trail.

That's the work of generations of indigenous trailblazers—coyotes, wolves, bobcats, or deer—that have their own network of highways to everyday destinations such as watering holes and shelter.

Notice that even free-roaming residents tend to stick to their established trails. As a visitor, you should consider these paths private driveways and steer clear.

Traffic Signs

Animal tracks may be one of the most exciting clues you'll find on the trail. They can reveal the size and species of the feet responsible, and perhaps even the circumstances in which they were made. Visiting a favorite grazing spot? Evading a predator? In hot pursuit?

Under the right conditions, even the smallest of creatures can leave a trail. More often, however, discernable tracks are subtle and incomplete. These are the prints your dog's nose can help you see, because most feet leave a distinct odor with every step.

Not all mammals make their way through the world with your particular style and grace. But each leaves behind an impression all his own.

Have Feet—Will Travel			
	SOLE WALKERS	TOE WALKERS	HOOF WALKERS	CLOVEN HOOF WALKERS
TOES PER FOOT	5	4 front, 5 rear, 2 or 4 dewclaws	1	4
FOOT	5 toe pads, 1 or more palm pads	4 or 5 toe pads, 1 palm pad	toe covered by hoof	2 middle toes covered with split hoof
FOOTPRINT	toes/claws often visible; palm pads occasionally	toes/palms/ claws visible; except in cats, which retract claws on the move	a well-defined, nearly circular print	hoof split in 2 "cleaves"; leaves parallel, ovallike prints
FOOT NOTES	tracks visible on most natural surfaces	typically fast runners	domesticated animals often leave shoe print	animals walk on two toes; outer toes are dewclaws
SOME MAMMALS THAT MAKE THEM	Humans, Bears, Dogs	Raccoons, Cats	Horses	Goats, Deer

CHAPTER 11

WHOA, ICK, AND OOPS!

What's Your Reaction When Nature Finds You?

A true wildlife encounter probably trumps any other surprise on the trail. But whether your first thoughts lean toward fascination or fear, your dog will be compelled by instinct. So it's your job as Alpha to control what happens next.

> One of the most reliable indicators of nearby wildlife is the animal at the end of your leash. Rigid posture, raised hackles (neck hair), ears perked forward, or stiff tail—any of these can indicate that your dog is on high alert.
>
> Watch your dog for changes in disposition on the trail, and consider what his body language is telling you. This is also a good time to hand the leash to the ultimate Alpha in your pack—someone who can keep your dog's excitement in check.

Hear Ye, Hear Ye

Nobody likes being snuck up on. So if you wander into the yard of a woodland neighbor, don't hang in the shadows. Ring the doorbell instead.

A freshly overturned log, possibly torn open by sharp claws, can alert you to a foraging bear in the area. Learning to recognize signs of wildlife can help you avoid anxious encounters on the trail (see Chapter 10).

Strike up a conversation with your pack; make noise and let the animal know that you're in the neighborhood. Most likely, he'll make himself scarce.

Coyotes are naturally shy but can become bold where unthinking hikers leave bread crusts, apple cores, and other choice snacks lying around. If you spot a coyote, slowly, noisily back away—if he hasn't already. Never turn your back on an animal and run.

If you suspect a bear in the area, don't wait for an actual sighting. Dial up the hubbub and gather your hiking party together to make yourselves larger than life. Walk with your arms in the air, waving your hat or a dry branch to communicate "large predator" rather than "small prey." Pull out your hiker's whistle and belt out a tune as you back away.

Never approach your subject, even to take pictures, and *never, ever feed the bears* (or the coyotes, or the groundhogs, or the squirrels . . .).

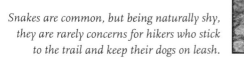

Snakes are common, but being naturally shy, they are rarely concerns for hikers who stick to the trail and keep their dogs on leash.

You leash your dog out of respect for every hiker's unalienable right to pursue happiness, without being pursued.

Steady as She Goes

The hiker who keeps his or her dog on leash can be confident that Rover is less likely to disturb/investigate fragile habitat, nesting sites, and occupied dens.

Look, but don't touch, and never let your curiosity draw you in—a protective parent could be nearby.

But what if you're the one with a locomotive of enthusiasm barreling down on you?

Stay Calm, Stay Put

Don't initiate a chase by running away. Innate, predatory instincts make the excitement of the chase irresistible to dogs.

This is a stressful encounter for your dog as well, especially since she's on leash. Show her some "Alpha-tude," talking quietly but firmly to reassure both dogs until the owner arrives.

More than likely, you'll find this domesticated wildlife to be in a gloriously good mood and really quite friendly.

Tick Talk

The wilderness experience doesn't always conclude at the end of the trail.

Check under your dog's collar, in the folds of your clothing, in your brother's hair—ticks are freeloaders that would like nothing better than to nose in on your vacation.

Don't give them an invitation in the first place. Always apply a topical flea and tick preventative to your pet well before your trip so that it will be active when you hit the trail. Headed into unfamiliar territory? Ask your doctor if he or she recommends vaccinating against regional hazards.

The only way to remove a tick safely is to grasp its mouth with tweezers right where it entered the skin. A slow, steady pull (don't bend, squeeze, or twist) completes the job. Ticks cannot be encouraged to simply let go. Petroleum jelly, alcohol, or a hot match will only agitate the tick, increasing the odds that pathogen-laden saliva will be released into the bite.

Where would you hide if you were itty-bitty and wanted to steal a meal? After a day on the trail, you should check those particular spots, and then every other place as well. Like most parasites, ticks can transmit some pretty nasty diseases.

Fortunately, when caught early and carefully removed, this tiny beastie is rarely a cause for concern.

Your best protection against pests on the trail is to wear light-colored pants (tucked into your socks), long sleeves, and a hat. Use a bug repellent with DEET. Then follow up with a good shower at home.

Once you've come clean, it's your dog's turn. Check your pal thoroughly, brushing his hair against the growth so that you can see down to the skin.

Again, it's important to fully vaccinate your pet and treat for fleas and ticks before you leave home. Insect repellents containing DEET or citronella can be harmful to your pet. Always ask your vet before using the family's bug repellents on your dog.

The Buzz about Heartworm Prevention

Obviously, dogs and their hiking partners aren't the only ones enjoying the great outdoors. Like ticks, mosquitoes are most active in the summer months and can carry a variety of diseases.

Heartworm larvae, transmitted by mosquito bites, pose a significant threat to your dog's health. Treatment after infection can be incredibly hard on your dog. Prevention is easy. Ask your vet to evaluate your dog's risk factors (including the area you'll hike) and recommend the best protection for your pal.

The Buzz about You

Mosquitoes consider any warm-blooded mammal a meal. Unfortunately, heavy breathing (lots of carbon dioxide), elevated body temperature, and body odor make hard-working hikers particularly enticing.

Wearing light-colored long sleeves and pants, as well as DEET repellent, and avoiding the hours between dusk and dawn all reduce the chance that you'll become a bite to eat.

Itching for Adventure?

Poison ivy and poison oak (also known as "leaves of three, let it be") grow in happy abundance just about anywhere a trail can take you. Unfortunately, your dog can spread the plants' poisons even farther.

Poison Ivy

- a shrub, creeping vine, or aerial-rooted tree climber
- three (sometimes five) ovallike, notched leaflets per stem
- often the first leaves to color in autumn (red and orange)
- a deciduous plant that winters as a hairy, rash-inducing vine

Poison Oak

- low-growing shrub
- three oak-shaped, glossy leaflets
- whitish flowers August–November
- a deciduous plant that winters as fuzzy, tan, rash-inducing twigs and branches

Poison Sumac

- leggy shrub grows in boggy areas, up to 15 feet
- 7–13 paired, smooth-edged leaflets, with one more at the tip of each stem

JUST 0.25 OUNCE OF URUSHIOL IS ENOUGH TO CAUSE A RASH IN EVERY PERSON ON EARTH!*

It takes little more than a wag to make these plants weep an oily tear potent enough to cause an angry, itchy rash. This natural irritant, urushiol, is easily absorbed into the skin. While it's not likely to find its way past a dog's fur (even on short-haired breeds), your pal can unwittingly snuggle sap onto you.

*Jim Dunphy, "Fast Facts" (Poison Ivy, Oak, & Sumac Information Center), (poisonivy.us)

If you suspect that your dog has tiptoed through the toxins, refrain from petting her until she's had a good, heavy soaping (be sure to wear gloves). Urushiol remains potent on gear, shoes, clothes, and, yes, on your dog's fur until it's washed away. In the meantime, douse her with plenty of cool water to dilute the oily residue. If you need to jump into the backseat with her for the ride home, get creative with what you've got. An XXL, long-sleeved shirt should fit both your dog and the task. On a hot day, take pity on your furry friend and wear the shirt yourself.

Keep off the Grass

The sly foxtail gives new meaning to the phrase "taking in the scenery." Not only will these golden-plumed grasses catch your eye, but they'll also catch your clothing, your shoe-

As the seed heads dry, foxtail grasses become dangerous to the pet that inhales, ingests, or merely steps on them.

strings, your skin, and, more sinister yet, your unsuspecting dog.

Foxtails are actually a variety of grasses with hard, barbed seeds that can hitch a ride on passersby. Their clever design encourages the plant's natural propagation, or reproduction. Unfortunately, these tenacious little seeds can create big problems for your pet. Sun-dried and sharp, a foxtail seed can find its way into your dog's body through any opening, and even through his skin. Once inside, it can travel practically anywhere, with any number of harmful bacteria in tow.

Steer clear of grasses in seed when possible, and check your dog's feet and fur at the end of each hike. Keep the hair on his feet trimmed short, and groom your dog often, so you can catch such problems before they take root.

"Leave It!"

If this command isn't in your dog's repertoire, it's worth learning. Once mastered, "Leave it!" can shield your homework from harm, as well as curb your dog's impulse to wear that sweet pile of scat he's just discovered on the trail.

Other temptations to be wary of are the random berry bush or mushroom, or the remains of a predator's meal.

Less obvious but equally problematic are those innocent-looking puddles and clear, "fresh" water.

Most natural water sources carry a bouquet of bacteria that can do a number on your dog's digestive tract, as well as yours. And not a bathroom in sight . . .

> **Visit your vet as soon as possible if you notice the following:**
> - licking, swelling, pain, or drainage, especially around the toes
> - immediate, uncontrollable sneezing, drainage, or bleeding from the nose
> - swelling and discharge from the eyes
> - head shaking and severe pain in the ears
> - forceful coughing or gagging
>
> **Never Attempt to Remove a Suspected Foxtail Yourself**

And Now for a Look at the Weather

The responsible hiker checks local weather forecasts and then packs for wide swings in temperature and conditions regardless.

Keep in mind that factors such as elevation, humidity, and wind will affect your comfort level throughout the day, especially for those of you wearing fur.

When You're Prepared for Anything, It's All Good

In the mountains, weather conditions can develop rapidly and unexpectedly. Avoid ridge hikes and balds when rain is expected (because of possible lightning), and carry a lightweight, plastic poncho to be ready for any unscheduled waterworks.

In regions with high humidity and higher daytime temperatures, you'll need to increase the amount of water you carry, for you and your dog. Likewise, hiking at higher elevations or in desert regions will mean long hours without shade. Time your hike for the coolest parts of the day.

Don't let a weather report cloud your sunny disposition. Keep extra layers of clothing and extra water in the trunk of your car, and don't forget to throw in the old towel—an indispensable device with nearly as many uses as duct tape.

> Before you start thinking that Mother Nature is out to get you, consider this: most of the natural nuisances mentioned in this chapter can be avoided simply by sticking to the trail.

> If you've planned ahead, the sun's burn will be slow to find you beneath your floppy hat and layers of sunscreen. But what about your dog? You are her most reliable SPF. Hairless, sparsely furred, and/or pink-nosed pups can burn just like you. Stick to the shade wherever possible. Ask your veterinarian to recommend an appropriate sunscreen after evaluating your dog's sensitivity.
>
> Don't forget your dog's feet. On hot days, parched earth and parking lots can feel like frying pans underfoot.

CHAPTER 12

Resting Your Dogs

All Trails Lead Back Home

Together, you rose to the challenge. You explored each turn of the trail with all of your combined ten senses. Finally back at the car, you're probably ready to crank the AC and cruise on home in time to hear the kibble rattle into the bowl. But that will have to wait.

The Hike Isn't Over until the Panting Ends

All good treks end in the quiet shade of a tree or a car's bumper (but not on paw-burning pavement). This is where you break out the stash in your trunk—water, snacks, and a towel for muddy paws—and bask in the glory of your accomplishments.

That's right, bask. Luxuriate. Slowly, wistfully, wallow. Wait.

You see, while your body has already begun its slide into deep relaxation, your dog's muscles are still hard at work with the business of bringing his body temperature back to normal. Offer your dog another drink and marvel at his stamina.

Water Works

If you're beginning to think that cool, clear water is a hiker's magic elixir, then you're getting the message.

Keep drinking water stowed in your car, so you will always have plenty of fresh water at the end of the trail.

EVEN THE CLEAREST LAKES AND STREAMS CARRY A VARIETY OF BELLY-WHOMPING BACTERIA. ALWAYS CARRY WATER FOR YOU AND YOUR PAL.

Panting is thirsty work, and your dog will need plenty of water to replace the moisture evaporating off his tongue. Offer your dog several short drinks instead of one long one. It will sit better with his tired tummy, and with the human who shares the backseat with him on the way home.

Treats All Around?

With all the calories burned on the trail, there are bound to be some tummies rumbling. Before you pass around the treats, however, you might want to assess your partner's ability to keep those cookies down. Some dogs are prone to becoming carsick under any circumstances. If it's been a particularly hot, active day, save the snacking until you return home.

CHECK FOR THORNS, BURRS, AND TICKS IN YOUR DOG'S FUR AND BETWEEN HER TOES DURING YOUR COOLDOWN.

The Alpha Dog's Post-Hike Checklist

Preserve the pack's health and well-being; check off these last concerns before heading home for the day.

- ❏ Has every one caught his or her breath?
- ❏ Had seconds on water?
- ❏ Eaten a light snack?
- ❏ Had time for stomachs to settle?
- ❏ Been checked for ticks?
- ❏ Passed a paws inspection?
- ❏ Made a final pit stop?
- ❏ Taken pictures?
- ❏ Re-stowed your camera?
- ❏ Packed out your trash?
- ❏ Left only footprints?

Home Again, Home Again

As you knock dirt from your boots at the back door, give yourself a quick recap of the day's highlights. Does it perhaps include a brush with poison ivy? Tick sightings? Muddy trail conditions or general "skunkiness"? It's likely that a warm soapy bath is in order for you and/or your dog.

If all that comes to mind is warmth and wags and happy trails, it's time to stretch out on the floor with your buddy and begin dreaming up your next big adventure.

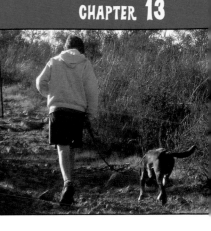

CHAPTER 13

KIBBLES AND BITS

Photos à la Fido

Your wilderness expeditions together will surely leave you with stories to tell. Plan ahead, and the photos you take will document every enthusiastic wag and achievement. Bone up on these photography tips, and your memories will stay colorful and sharp for years.

- Pull your camera out early and often.

- Narrate your adventure with pictures; photograph your pet in front of each new trailhead and attraction.

- Try looking at the world from a dog's-eye view to add drama and humor to your tale.

- Shoot more than just the scenery—catch your pooch and your people in action, and hand off the camera frequently so that you're in lots of photos yourself.

- To make those awesome vistas more expansive, include your dog in the foreground to emphasize the grand scale of things.

- Choose your camera angle so that the sun won't shine into your subjects' eyes or your camera's lens.

- Wear light, bright colors. Color adds to any photo and makes you more visible on the trail.

- Center your primary subject while focusing, and then frame the shot how you like.

- To get that perfect tilt of the head, give a little squeak, hiccup, or chirp to pique your dog's interest.

- If you want a shot from the car, clear it with the driver first. Then roll down the window so that you're not shooting through a haze of dog drool and nose prints.

- Hiking with your camera in hand can be dangerous; carrying it around your neck or hooked to your belt makes it accessible.

Digital cameras give you the freedom to shoot and shoot. But great pictures can be coaxed from convenient, disposable cameras as well. Just focus on what these cameras shoot best—medium distance, outdoor shots. Panoramic photos produce wide photos but not the eyes-wide vista of real life. Have your group strike a pose in the foreground, and their wide smiles will document some of that drama.

Links to the Outside World

Nature Find—Find trails, parks, outdoor activities by zip code, articles, a kids' page, and more, all courtesy of the National Wildlife Federation . . . **nwf.org/naturefind**

U.S. National Forests—Dog-friendly trails wind through many of our national forests. Find one near you . . . **www.fs.fed.us/recreation/map/state_list**

U.S. National Parks—Dogs have limited access to trails, so check here for park-specific regulations before you go; these parks are well worth the trip, even if Fido has to stay home . . . **nps.gov/findapark**

State Parks—A list of the country's state parks; trail descriptions and specific information for individual parks; directions . . . **stateparks.com**

Appalachian Trail—This hike travels through eight national forests, 14 states, and 2,179 miles; find maps and news; search site for "kids" and "dogs" . . . **appalachiantrail.org**

Trails and Reviews—Paying subscribers can find directions to a world of trails, with descriptions and difficulty ratings . . . **trails.com**

Leave No Trace—Practices for low-impact hiking and camping; volunteer opportunities; the Bigfoot Challenge . . . **lnt.org**

Hike with Your Dog—"Tail friendly" trails; hiking and camping tips; dog-friendly beaches . . . **hikewithyourdog.com**

Dog Parks—A listing of major dog parks by state; visit your closest park for pre-hike conditioning and socialization . . . **dogparksusa.com**

The Trail Hound's website— a place to share your own dog-powered adventures, post dog pics, and more . . . HikingWithDogs.net

CHAPTER 14

A Trail Hound's Journal

Date	We Sniffed out This Great Spot	And This Is What Got Our Tails Waggin'

Date	We Sniffed out This Great Spot	And This Is What Got Our Tails Waggin'

Date	We Sniffed out This Great Spot	And This Is What Got Our Tails Waggin'

Date	We Sniffed out This Great Spot	And This Is What Got Our Tails Waggin'

Date	We Sniffed out This Great Spot	And This Is What Got Our Tails Waggin'

backcountry   *n.* any area that is remote and undeveloped, often used interchangeably with the word *wilderness* (p. 26)

bald   *n.* a mountain summit or crest covered by thick native grasses or shrubs (p. 54)

blaze   *n.* a mark painted onto a rock or tree, or carved into a tree's bark, that indicates the path of some trails, especially at intersections, over rough terrain, or where the path may become covered in snow (p. 27)

brachycephalic   *adj.* having a relatively short, wide head—as do the pug, bulldog, and Shih Tzu—with the nose to match (p. 7)

bouldering   *v.* climbing or traveling over boulders and rocky terrain rather than on an established path or trail (p. 9)

buck rub   *n.* scarred tree bark and limbs, 5–8 feet off the ground, created when male deer rub their antlers to mark territory, scratch an itch, or polish newly matured antlers; also known as a deer rub (p. 43)

cairn   *n.* a pile of stones set as a trail marker; cairns should be left undisturbed so that future travelers can easily navigate the path (p. 27)

Canidae family   *n.* the mammal group that includes dogs, wolves, jackals, coyotes, and foxes (p. 3)

choke chain   *n.* a dog collar designed to correct unwanted behavior during training; choke chains are inappropriate in the woods, as they pose a choking risk should the dog become entangled (pp. 10 and 15)

ecosystem   *n.* a group of organisms and the environment that they inhabit and depend on (pp. 28 and 42)

eye shine   *n.* the glowing effect seen when light hits the eyes of certain mammals, including dogs; light bouncing off of a reflective layer of cells called the tapetum in these animals' eyes (p. 39)

game trail   *n.* an informal path established by the routine traffic patterns of animals in their wild habitat; such trails usually lead to fresh water, good hunting, and trusted shelter (p. 46)

hackles   *n.* the hair located along the length of a dog's backbone, from the neck to the base of the tail, that stands on end in response to overexcitement, fear, or aggression (p. 48)

indigenous   *adj.* naturally occurring, living, or growing in a certain area; not transplanted or imported from somewhere else (p. 46)

low-impact hiking *n.* "enjoying without destroying"; an approach to outdoor activities that emphasizes planning, preparation, and discipline to keep human activities from impacting the natural environment (p. 26, 30)

molt *v.* to shed feathers, hair, or skin periodically or seasonally (p. 44)

nictitating membrane *n.* also known as the haw; is essentially a third, somewhat transparent eyelid that keeps the eye moistened and clean (p. 40)

owl pellet *n.* a regurgitated wad of fur and bone; the indigestible parts of an owl's meal (p. 42)

predatory *adj.* characteristic of animals that survive by preying on other animals (pp. 3 and 49)

pheromones *n.* a unique mix of chemicals secreted by the body and picked up and analyzed by a dog's super-sensitive nose; pheromones help dogs identify others of their species or specific pack members and humans (p. 32)

regurgitate *v.* to cough up partially digested or indigestible food from the stomach; some parents in nature regurgitate to supply nutritious, easily digested baby food to young offspring (p. 42)

scat *n.* wild-animal poop; a telltale sign of wildlife, and the nature of its diet (p. 41)

scree *n.* loose rock debris covering a slope or piled at the base of a steep incline (p. 9)

shed *n.* material naturally cast off as an animal molts, important to the forest food chain and cycle of life; a sign of wildlife in the area (p. 44)

snag *n.* a dead but upright tree; an important source of habitat for birds, small mammals, and insects; a great source of food for birds and bears (p. 44)

switchbacks *n.* a section of trail that cuts back and forth across steep terrain to make it more easily hiked; also designed to minimize erosion (p. 27)

tapetum *n.* a thin layer of reflective cells in a dog's eyes that allow it to see well in dim light; results in the visual phenomenon called eye shine (p. 39)

territorial *adj.* protective with regard to habitat, resources, or pack (p. 3)

urushiol *n.* the toxic sap of poison ivy, oak, and sumac that causes a rash upon contact with the skin (p. 52)

parks, 58
resting your, 55–56
sunscreen for, 54
tongues of, 34
traits, 31–40
types, and appropriate hike, 7–13
wildlife hazards, 48–54
dog crates, 23
dogfights, 12, 25
dog obedience
  barking on command, 8
  on hiking trails, 25–30
  practicing skills, 3
  training collars, 10
dog backpacks, 11, 18, 19
dog tags, 16
dog waste, cleaning up, 28

E

ear leather, 36
ears, dog, 35–37
ear types, 36
ecosystem, 28, 42, 64
elevation gain, and trail difficulty, 12
emergencies
  confrontations with other dogs, 12
  first-aid kit, 20
endurance, 11
energetic dogs, hiking with, 12
equipment. See also specific type
  for dogs, 10, 11, 14–18
  for people, 19
essentials for hiking with dogs, 14
essentials for people, 19

evolution of dogs, 2–3
exercise
  benefits of, 5, 7
  dog's need for, 4
  for dog walkers, 19
  overdoing, 11, 18
  for overweight dogs, 9, 12
  for pups and seniors, 7
eye shine, 39, 64
eyesight of dogs, 38–40

F

fatigue, 8, 18
feces, 17, 28, 41
first-aid kit
  checklist, 20
  poison ivy, 52
  tick removal, 50
fitness, assessing your dog's, 6, 18, 19
flea and tick prevention, 21, 50
food
  not sharing with your dog, 19
  on the road, 24, 56
  on the trail, 19, 56
footprints, animal (table), 47
foxtails, 53
furry dogs, hiking with, 8, 9

G

game trails, 45, 64
garbage, packing out, 17, 30
gear. See equipment
glossary, 64–65

anairam_zeravla/morgueFile.com: 8 top. antalvespo/morgueFile.com: 12 bottom. Angelo Arcadi/iStockphoto.com: 14 top. Michael L. Baird, flickr.bairdphotos.com: 8 center, 22 bottom. Scott Bauer/USDA Agricultural Research Service: 50. T. Travis Brown: 41 left, 41 center, 42 center, 45 bottom. Travis Bryant: 3 top. brycesteiner/morgueFile. com: 38 top. Eunice Chang: 51 bottom. clconroy/morgueFile.com: 27 top, 45 center right (raccoon). click/morgueFile.com: 45 top. cohdra/morgueFile.com: 27 bottom left. Tudor Costache: 12 center, 35 top. dawnsarro/morgueFile.com: 21 top left. dpawatts/ morgueFile.com: 45 center left (bird). Jeremy Edwards/iStockphoto.com: 22 top. el_alf/ morgueFile.com: 46 bottom. FreeDigitalPhotos.net: 25 bottom, 36 top left. gaspr13/ iStockphoto.com: 19 top. Lewis Glick/USFWS: 47 center far left. gracey/morgueFile. com: 45 center top right (eggshell). greenfinger/morgueFile.com: 57 top left. Bill Grove/ iStockphoto.com: 28 top. Ryan Hagerty/USFWS: 45 center (rabbit). hamper/ morgueFile.com: 47 top. Amber Kaye Henderson: 9 bottom. holder/morgueFile.com: 47 center left. jade/morgueFile.com: 4 center. jdurham/morgueFile.com: 20 bottom, 24 top. John Joh: 31 top. julesinky/morgueFile.com: 7 top. Gary Kramer/USFWS: 2 top. lemort/morgueFile.com: 10 top. lisasolonynko/morgueFile.com: 7 center top, 34 bottom. MacKinnon Photography: 17 top. Andrew Magill: 11 bottom. manicmorff/ morgueFile.com: 42 top. Joe Martin/USFWS: 45 center bottom left (squirrel). Steve Maslowski/USFWS: 43 top. mconnors/morgueFile.com: 52 bottom. mdf/ WikimediaCommons: 27 center top. mettem/morgueFile.com: 27 center bottom. Robert H. Mohlenbrock © USDA-NRCS PLANTS Database/USDA SCS. 1991. *Southern wetland flora: Field office guide to plant species.* South National Technical Center, Fort Worth: 52 top left, 52 center top, 52 top right. nazka200z/morgueFile.com: 8 bottom. Nova Development Corporation: 6 top, 11 top, 13 top, 21 top right, 22 center top, 36 bottom right, 51 top. pannan/morgueFile.com: 9 center. Dot Paul/USDA Natural Resources Conservation Service: 46 top. paulabflat/morgueFile.com: 36 bottom left. penywise/ morgueFile.com: 26 top. pixelrave/morgueFile.com: 49 center right. Don Poggensee/ USDA Natural Resources Conservation Service: 49 bottom. ppdigital/morgueFile.com: 34 center. quidp/morgueFile.com: 5. ricetek/morgueFile.com: 45 center top left (nest). Mark Robinson: 49 center left. schick/morgueFile.com: 10 center, 33 bottom. G. J. Searle Jr.: 74. Maggie Smith/FreeDigitalPhotos.net: 35 bottom. John Stehn/ USFWS: 44 bottom. Gordon Surratt: 26 bottom right. taliesin/morgueFile.com: 9 top, 14 bottom, 34 top, 48 bottom, 49 top. tangle_eye/morgueFile.com: 53 top right. Theilr: 7 center bottom, 25 top. Steve Thompson/USFWS: 48 top. Emmett Tullos III: 39 top. USDA Natural Resources Conservation Service: 46 center right. USFWS: 42 bottom. Jeff Vanuga/USDA Natural Resources Conservation Service: 43 center. xandert/ morgueFile.com: 13 bottom, 23 center left, 40 center, 44 center. xpSquid/morgueFile. com: 47 center far right. Stephanie Zens: 54.

For outdoor adventurers who hike, fish, kayak, cross-country ski, or mountain bike in the backcountry, a GPS receiver can help them reach their destination and return safely—but only if they know how to use it! Here is the guide to getting the most out of a GPS receiver, from basic consumer advice to advanced techniques. It even includes fun solo and team games that utilize GPS. Starting with essential definitions such as UTM coordinate systems, position formats, and map datums—and moving on to creating waypoints and using your GPS with a computer—this succinct book teaches you what you really need to know for outdoor GPS use, including basic map-and-compass skills and primitive navigation techniques that you can use if your GPS unit fails.

Advanced techniques, such as creating custom maps, are also covered, and new technologies, including how to use GPS-enabled mobile phones (and why they won't always find your position in the wilderness) and how to use GPS with Google Earth and Google Maps, are discussed. With years of experience as a GPS instructor, author Stephen Hinch is well-versed in all aspects of navigation and GPS use, and he covers them all in a jargon-free, easy-to-follow style.

Outdoor Navigation with GPS
Author ......Stephen W. Hinch
ISBN 978-0-89997-650-1
Price $17.95

About Stephen W. Hinch

Stephen Hinch has taught courses in GPS navigation to police and fire personnel, park rangers, search-and-rescue staff, and recreational outdoor enthusiasts since 1998. When he was young, his avid rockhound parents would pack up the family and head out to remote desert locations in search of semiprecious stones nearly every weekend. These desert explorations honed his navigational skills and taught him the importance of not getting lost.

Trained as an electrical engineer, Hinch has more than 30 years of experience in upper-level management in the high-tech industry, with three patents to his name. He maintains an active author blog about GPS technology on Amazon.com.

wildernesspress.com

Small and lightweight, each guide in the *Easy Hikes Close to Home* series features approximately 20 hikes. With trails personally tested by the authors, these guides include at-a-glance details (such as length, water required, trail traffic and surface, and wheelchair accessibility), GPS trailhead coordinates, directions, and clear maps.

MENASHA RIDGE PRESS

Easy Hikes
Close to Home

SEATTLE

ANDREW WEBER/BRYCE STEVENS

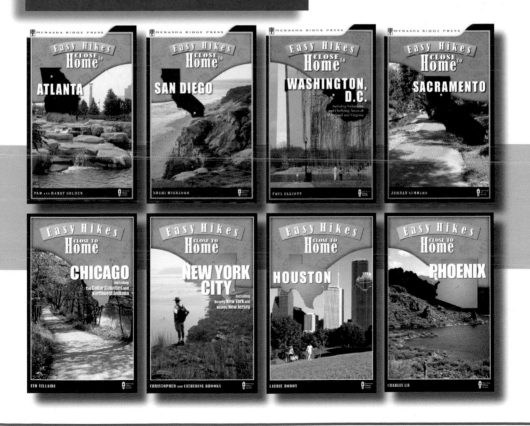

"Most of the self-confidence I had as a young teen, I picked up along a hiking trail. The rest probably came from the slobbering affections of the family dog," says author Ellen Eastwood.

It's no surprise, then, that a lifetime of dog ownership and miles of wilderness trails led Eastwood to create *The Trail Hound's Handbook*. With a journalism degree from the University of North Carolina at Chapel Hill, Eastwood has more than 15 years of advertising and newsletter copy writing and design experience. Years in the classroom with preschool and school-age children, and her current position as mother of four (two children and two dogs), further prepared her for writing this book.

Eastwood and her pack currently reside in Westlake Village, California, surrounded by the rugged Santa Monica Mountains. When she's not outside with her dogs, she is volunteering at her kids' schools; working on her new website, **HikingWithDogs.net**; or playing basketball in a local women's league.